THE
BIODEGRADABLE
JOKE BOOK

THE BIODEGRADABLE JOKE BOOK

Teresa Green

with cartoons by
Peter Poole

MAMMOTH

First published 1990 by Mammoth
an imprint of Mandarin Paperbacks
Michelin House, 81 Fulham Road, London SW3 6RB

Mandarin is an imprint of the Octopus Publishing Group

ISBN 0 7497 0341 5

A CIP catalogue record for this title
is available from the British Library

Printed in Great Britain
by Cox & Wyman Ltd, Reading, Berkshire

INTRODUCTION

BOY: Dad, what's nuclear fission?

FATHER: Er, I'm afraid I don't know anything about atomic energy.

BOY: Well, can you tell me about global warming and the greenhouse effect?

FATHER: Sorry, son, I don't really know much about that sort of thing.

BOY: Oh. Can you tell me about eco-friendly household products, unleaded petrol, and the destruction of tropical rain forests?

FATHER: Mmm, you've got me there, I'm afraid.

BOY: You don't mind me asking you all these questions about the environment, do you Dad?

FATHER: Of course not, son. You have to ask questions if you want to learn anything....

It's a funny old world, isn't it? But I tell you what, if we're not careful it's going to be a funny old *dead* world. We live surrounded by seas that are dying, polluted with everything from nuclear waste to contaminated sewage sludge and every kind of industrial pollution. Many of our beaches are classified as health hazards. A large number of our rivers are thick with scum and effluent.

But that's not all. Around the world, an estimated 100 species of life are being eliminated every day. Chimneys continue to belch out sulphur dioxide even though we know that acid rain is killing Europe's forests and lakes. And we're still building nuclear power stations, despite the awful warning of Chernobyl.

What's the world coming to? you might ask. The answer is: a very sticky end if we don't do something about it. Our planet is in a sad state. We've got to cheer it up. So while you're enjoying the jokes in this book, think about things and ask yourself how *you* can help.

It's up to all of us to do our bit, or the earth will die.

And that would be no laughing matter.

THE
BIODEGRADABLE
JOKE BOOK

Environmentally Friendly Jokes

Who sings and helps insulate the home from draughts?
Julio Doubleglasias.

How do Red Indians send secret messages?
With smokeless fuel.

What has two legs, one wheel, and stinks to high heaven?
A barrowload of manure.

What's the best way to save water?
Dilute it.

What is wind?
Air in a hurry.

What keeps sheep warm in winter?
Central bleating.

Did you hear about the girl who bought a pair of
biodegradable paper knickers?
She didn't like them; they were tear-able.

Did you hear the Department of Energy is
experimenting with wind power?
They all eat ten tins of baked beans a day.

What colour is the wind?
Blew.

Where was the Antarctic Treaty signed?
At the bottom.

What's renewable and derived from wind, sun, tides, waves and biofuels, in just three letters?
N–R–G

How do you address a female health inspector?
'Hi, Jean.'

Unmentionable Biodegradables....

What is an ig?
An Eskimo house without a loo.

What kind of tree grows near volcanoes?
A lava tree (lavatory).

What do men do standing up, women do sitting down, and dogs do on three legs?
Shake hands.

What's brown and steaming and comes out of Cowes?
The Isle of Wight ferry.

What's brown and sounds like a bell?
Dung.

What happened to the farmer who sat under the cow?
He got a pat on the head.

1ST MAN: I've just bought my wife a bottle of toilet water for £20.
2ND MAN: £20! You could have come round to our house and had some out of our toilet for nothing.

Why did Captain Kirk pee on the ceiling?
To boldly go where no man had gone before.

Which French painter was short but very clean?
Two-loos Lautrec.

What kind of nut do you find in the loo?
A pee-nut!

What's famous and lives in lavatories?
Someone flushed with success.

What's brown and causes panic in a convent?
A raised lavatory seat.

1ST WOMAN: We've been in Paris a week and
we haven't visited the Louvre yet.
2ND WOMAN: I expect it's the change in the
water.

Knock, knock.
– *Who's there?*
Butter.
– *Butter who?*
Butter be quick, I need the toilet urgently!

Who dashed around the desert on a camel,
carrying a bedpan?
Florence of Arabia.

1ST GIRL: You need to be a good singer in our house.
2ND GIRL: Why's that?
1ST GIRL: There's no lock on the loo door.

Knock, knock.
– *Who's there?*
Luke.
– *Luke who?*
Luke through the keyhole and you'll see auntie on the toilet.

What happened when the boy put a firework down the toilet?
Nothing — it was just a flash in the pan.

Thieves stole a lorry last night that was delivering new toilet seats to the police station. Detectives say they have nothing to go on.

What was the most difficult deed for a knight in armour?
Going to the lavatory.

Non-Biodegradable Jokes

What gets larger the more you subtract?
A hole in the ozone layer.

If a red house is made of red bricks, and a blue house is made of blue bricks, what is a greenhouse made of?
Glass.

What's Green politics?
A parrot that's swallowed an alarm clock.

What is the future of coal?
Smoke.

What made the chimney ill?
It had a touch of flue.

What's the dirtiest word in the world?
Pollution.

What did the big chimney say to the small chimney?
'You're far too young to smoke.'

What did one oil slick say to the other oil slick?
'Oil see you again.'

What's wet, black, floats on water, and shouts 'Knickers!'
Crude oil.

What's wet, black, floats on water and shouts 'Underwear!'
Refined oil.

Did you hear about the millionaire who hated washing?
He was filthy rich.

**Anti-Social Aerosols Attack
Atmosphere Abominably**

PITT: What's the smelliest part of the human body, Fitt?
FITT: I'd say the arm, Pitt.

Did you hear the joke about the aerosol deodorant?
Never mind, it stinks!

What do you get if you cross an aerosol deodorant with a boomerang?
A bad smell you can't get rid of.

What did one eye say to the other?
'Between us is something that smells.'

What do you call an old aerosol deodorant?
Ex-stinked.

What do you get if you cross an aerosol
deodorant with a bear?
Winnie the Pooh.

What do you get if you cross an aerosol
deodorant with a horse?
Whinny the Pooh.

What do you get if you cross an aerosol deodorant with a hedgehog?
A porcupong.

What contest do aerosol deodorants enter?
The Eurovision Pong Contest.

How many aerosol deodorants do you need to make a big stink?
Just a phew.

Greenhouse Gathers Gases:
Globe Gets Gradually Grottier

What's hot and moves at 100 mph?
A person running a temperature.

What comes out of the washing machine at 100
degrees centigrade?
Hot pants!

What do you get if you cross a shark with a
snowman?
Frostbite.

Knock, knock.
– *Who's there?*
Martini.
– *Martini who?*
Martini hand is frozen.

What's blue, worn over a shirt, and bursts into flames easily?
A blazer.

24

Which animal would you like to be in a cold climate?
A little otter.

What do you get if you cross cold weather with bandages?
A frostaid kit.

Why is it hard to keep a secret in winter?
Because your teeth chatter.

What did Big Chief Running Water call his two sons?
Hot and Cold.
And what did he call his third son?
Little Drip.

Why is draughts a dangerous game?
Because you could catch a chill.

What stays hot in the fridge?
Mustard.

How do ants keep warm in winter?
Antifreeze.

What's got four wheels and sizzles when it's hot?
An old banger.

Why do you feel cold when you lose your two front teeth?
No central eating.

What lives in winter, dies in summer and grows with its roots upwards?
An icicle.

How do misers keep warm when it's cold?
They sit around a candle.

How do misers keep warm when it's *very* cold?
They light it.

Rivers

What has a mouth, and a fork, yet never eats?
A river

Why should you never swim in the river in Paris?
Because to do so would be in Seine.

What parts of the river can be eaten?
The source (sauce) and the currents (currants).

What does a rower drink at bedtime?
Oar-licks.

What has four eyes and runs over 2000 miles?
The Mississippi river (Four is).

What is denial?
An Egyptian river.

What's the speed limit in Egypt?
30 Niles per hour.

TEACHER: What do you know about the Dead Sea?
PUPIL: Dead? I didn't even know it was ill.

How much fuel does a pirate ship use?
About 15 miles to the galleon.

Why did the sailor grab a cake of soap when his ship was sinking?
He hoped he would be washed ashore.

Where do fish wash?
In a river basin.

TEACHER: What do you call the small rivers
that flow into the river Nile?
PUPIL: Juveniles!

What goes into the water pink and comes out
blue?
A swimmer on a cold day.

What is the difference between a pound and the
ocean?
Weight and sea!

What lives in the sea and pulls teeth?
The dental sturgeon.

What lies at the bottom of the sea and shivers?
A nervous wreck.

What is the most untidy part of a ship?
The officers' mess.

What does the sea say to the sand?
Not a lot – it mostly waves.

If a Red Indian falls into the Black Sea, what does he become?
Wet.

What part of a ship is strict?
The stern part.

What lives under the sea and carries lots of people?
An octobus.

Water Wastage Wallops World!

How did the girl's father know she hadn't had a bath?
She forgot to wet the soap.

What can fall on water without getting wet?
A shadow.

What's the best way to keep water out of the home?
Don't pay the Water Rates.

Which city has the cleanest people?
Bath.

What can run across the floor but has no legs?
Water.

How do you spy on the Water Board?
Tap the phone.

What is the formula for water?
HIJKLMNO (H to O: H_2O)

Do you always bath in dirty water?
It wasn't dirty when I got in.

Wicked Wood Wasters Wither World

Did you hear about the wooden car with a wooden engine and wooden wheels?
It wooden go.

What's wooden, howls, and is dangerous?
A timber wolf.

What's wooden and smells?
A high chair.

Why did the wally abandon his attempt to cross the Atlantic ocean on a plank of wood?
He couldn't find a plank long enough.

'I'm looking for a man with a wooden leg called Johnson.'
'What's his real leg called?'

Why were the seven planks of wood standing in a circle?
They were having a board meeting.

What cuts wood and worries?
A fretsaw.

Why is the Queen like a length of wood?
Because she is a ruler.

What is the best kind of wood for making deckchairs
Beech.

What's the best place to buy exotic plants?
At a jungle sale.

What's an icon?
The fruit of an Australian oak tree.

What is the difference between a train and a tree?
One leaves its shed, the other sheds its leaves.

How do you get a one-armed wally out of a tree?
Wave to him.

Which tree do you find after a fire?
The ash.

What swings through the trees carrying a briefcase?
A branch manager.

Which tree is the most well-liked?
The poplar.

Which is the oldest tree of them all?
The elder.

What do you get if you cross a calculator with an acorn?
An oak tree with square roots.

Did you hear about the wally who hurt himself raking leaves?
He fell out of the tree.

What do you get hanging from trees?
Sore arms.

What is black, out of its mind, and sits in trees?
A raven lunatic.

Bilious Burgers Bring Burps, Burn Brazil!

What do you get if you cross a house with a quarter pound of mince?
A homeburger

What do you get if you cross a church choir with a quarter pound of mince?
A hymnburger.

'Waiter, will my hamburger be long?'
'No sir, it will be round and flat.'

What do you get if you cross a bee with half a kilo of mince?
Humburgers.

What's hot, greasy and steals cattle?
A beef burglar.

What's the best thing to put into a hamburger?
Your teeth.

WAITER: We have everything on the menu.
DINER: So I see. Kindly bring me a clean one.

There were two provisions shops next door to one another. One put up a sign:
WE SELL OUR BATTERY-REARED EGGS, SOFT CHEESE AND PATÉ TO THE QUEEN.
The next day the other put up a sign:
GOD SAVE THE QUEEN.

DINER: How often do you change the tablecloths in this establishment?
WAITER: I don't know, sir, I've only been here six months.

1ST BOY: I know a café where we can eat dirt cheap.
2ND BOY: But who wants to eat dirt?

'Are you sure this ham is cured? It tastes as if it's still sick!'

'Waiter, what's wrong with this fish?'
'Long time, no sea, sir.'

What's yellow, brown and hairy?
Cheese on toast dropped on the carpet.

Did you hear the joke about the three eggs?
Two bad.

CORONER: And what were your wife's last words, sir?
MAN: They were: 'I don't see how they can make a profit selling this chicken at 2p a pound.'

Energy

What did the robot say when it ran out of electricity?
'AC come, AC go.'

What did the mother robot say to the little robot when he came home after midnight?
'Wire you insulate?'

What did the wall say to the plug?
'Socket to me, baby.'

What did the electricity meter say to the 10p piece?
'Glad you dropped in, I was just going out.'

What did the robot say to her boyfriend?
'I love you watts and watts....'

What would you do if you swallowed a lightbulb?
Use a candle instead.

Why did the baker get an electric shock?
He stood on a bun and the current ran up his leg.

What's the most shocking city in the world?
Electri-city.

What do you get if you cross William the Conqueror with a power station?
An electricity bill.

What's black, hairy and surrounded by water?
An oil wig.

How can you tell a wally on an oil rig?
He's the one throwing bread to the helicopters.

What happens when you sleep under a car?
You wake up oily in the morning.

What did the coke sing to the coal?
'*What kind of fuel am I?*'

Who is in charge of all the pits in England?
Old King Cole Miner.

Nuclear Nasties

What do you get if you swallow uranium?
Atomic ache.

* *Nuclear Energy* by Molly Cule
* *Useless Power* by Alec Tricity

What do nuclear scientists do on holiday?
They go fission.

What did the loony nuclear physicist try to grow in his greenhouse?
An atomic energy plant.

TEACHER: What is an atom?
PUPIL: The man who lived in the Garden of Eden with Eve.

What is blonde, sings and is
very dangerous?
Olivia Neutron-Bomb.

What's got two wheels, a bell and waves
a banner?
A CND Raleigh.

What's always served in a nuclear power station canteen?
Fission chips.

What is round and brown and travels great distances?
An intercontinental ballistic rissole.

What is long and yellow and travels great distances?
An intercontinental banana missile.

Travelling Tourists Threaten Terrain

What is the difference between a jumbo jet and
a lemon?
A lemon can't fly to New York without refuelling.

Where do cows go for their holidays?
Moo York.

What's small and grey and has a trunk?
A mouse going on holiday.

Where's Yarmouth?
Same place as yours – under my nose.

Who is blonde, sings and lives in
South America?
Bolivia Newton-John.

What do you call an Irish Apache?
Tom O'Hawk.

What do you give a seasick elephant?
Plenty of room.

Where do ghosts go for their holidays?
Goole.

Where do Egyptian mummies go for
their holidays?
The Dead Sea.

How do you contact the police
in Australia?
Dial 666.

What's tall and wobbly and stands in the middle of Paris?
The Trifle Tower

'Mummy, mummy, I don't want to go to America!'
'Shut up and keep swimming.'

NERVOUS AIR PASSENGER: How often do planes of this type crash?
AIR HOSTESS: Only once, madam.

What's the best place to hold a party in California?
San Frandisco.

What's the cheapest way to get to China?
Be born there.

Where are the Andes?
At the end of the wristies.

What's purple, juicy and 2000 miles long?
The Grape Wall of China.

Where do ghosts swim in North America?
Lake Eerie.

What monster became President
of France?
Charles de Ghoul.

How do you contact the police in Germany?
Dial nein, nein, nein.

What stands in the middle of Paris and smells nice?
The Eiffel Flower.

Who ruled Gaul and kept catching colds?
Julius Sneezer.

How was the Roman Empire cut in half?
With a pair of Caesars.

Which island is six-sided?
Cuba.

Why is Europe like a frying-pan?
Because it has Greece at the bottom.

What do you get if you cross the Atlantic Ocean
with the Titanic?
Halfway.

PASSENGER: Guard, how long will the next
train be?
GUARD: About six carriages, sir.

What make the Tower of Pisa lean?
It never eats.

What is a Laplander?
A clumsy person on a bus.

What is the coldest country in the world?
Chile.

What kind of ears do trains have?
Engineers.

MAN: A return ticket, please.
RAILWAY CLERK: Where to?
MAN: Why, back here of course!

'One of my ancestors fell at Waterloo.'
'Really? Which platform?'

What transport is safest in a storm?
A bus – it has a conductor.

What's big and hairy and flies
at 2000 mph?
King Kongcorde.

What's sweet, clever and travels
by Underground?
A tube of Smarties.

What's big, red and airy?
A bus with its windows open.

What happened when the wheel
was invented?
There was a revolution.

Why can't a steam engine sit down?
Because it has a tender behind.

Why couldn't the bicycle stand up?
Because it was tyred.

What waves a magic wand and goes from Dover
to Calais?
A cross-Channel fairy.

What's big, red and lies upside down in the
gutter?
A dead bus.

What bus crossed the Atlantic Ocean
in 1492?
Christopher Colum-bus.

Who didn't invent the aeroplane?
The Wrong brothers.

What's a twack?
Something a twain runs on.

How do you spot a wally in a car wash?
He's the one on the motorbike.

What kind of motorbike would
a comedian ride?
A Yama-ha-ha.

What travels on water and land, sucking up all the dirt?
A Hoovercraft.

What travels along the riverbed at 100 mph?
A motorpike.

What rides along the clothes line at 100 mph?
Honda pants!

What do you call a vicar on a motorbike?
Rev.

Paper Plastic Packaging
Plunders Planet

What's wrapped in clingfilm and lives
in Paris?
The lunchpack of Notre Dame.

What do you carry an Indian takeaway home in?
A curryer bag.

What is the difference between an empty beer
can and a daft Dutchman?
*One is a hollow cylinder, the other is
a silly Hollander.*

Why did the tin whistle?
Because the tin can.

Why is it nice to be a baby?
Because it is a nappy time.

'Doctor, Doctor, my hair is falling out! Can you give me something for it?'
'Yes, here's a paper bag.'

What's wrapped in tin foil and has an
ON/OFF switch?
A TV dinner.

What has a neck but cannot swallow?
A bottle.

Why don't polar bears eat penguins?
Because they can't get the wrappers off.

Did you hear about the cowboy with
paper trousers?
He was arrested for rustling.

What's plastic, works on batteries, and counts
cattle?
A cow-culator.

Did you hear about the plastic surgeon who sat by the fire?
He melted.

Rubbish!

* *The Dustman's Story* by M T Binns

What is a lazy person's favourite hobby?
Sitting in a corner collecting dust.

Did you hear about the blind and deaf skunk?
Its best friend was a dustbin.

'Doctor, doctor, my wife keeps putting me in the dustbin.'
'Don't talk rubbish.'

Do litter collectors have to be trained?
No, they pick it up as they go along.

Why will the dustbin collector never accept an invitation?
Because he is a refuse man.

'Mummy, Mummy, why can't we
have a dustbin?'
'Shut up and keep chewing.'

Why is a belt like a dustbin lorry?
*Because it goes round and gathers
up the waste.*

What's got four wheels and flies?
A dustcart.

Noxious Noise Niggles Neighbours Needlessly

What's the definition of noise?
Two skeletons jiving in a biscuit tin.

TEACHER: Quiet! Order, everyone, order!
PUPIL: Okay, I'll have a large burger with fries...

Why is whispering illegal?
Because it's not allowed.

What's black and white and noisy?
A zebra with a drumkit.

What did the angry passenger on the aeroplane say to the noisy child?
'Why don't you go and play outside?'

Why did the ocean roar?
Because it had crabs in its bed.

What do you get if you cross a French emperor with a ton of TNT?
Napoleon Blownapart!

What's red and shouts, 'Knickers!'?
Little Rude Riding Hood.

What goes 'MOOB! MOOB!'?
Concorde flying backwards.

Knock, Knock.
– *Who's there?*
Noise.
– *Noise who?*
Noise to see you!

Why wouldn't the ghetto blaster work after the steam roller had gone over it?
Because the batteries were flat.

Reduce Rampaging Roads – Rather, Raise Rambling

What's black, lives in Scotland, and knew Eve?
Tarmacadam.

What's grey and white and runs from London to Scotland without moving?
The M1.

What is a road hog?
A pig-headed driver.

Where's Spaghetti Junction?
Just past-a Birmingham.

What do you call a road that has diamond-studded cats' eyes?
A jewel carriageway.

What's green and has two lanes?
A dual cabbage-way.

Why did the hedgehog cross the road?
To see his flat-mate.

A lorry carrying hair-restorer has crashed on the M5. Police are combing the area.

What weighs many tons, travels much too fast on the motorway, and drips?
An articulated lolly.

How do you avoid that run-down feeling?
Look both ways before crossing.

'Do you know someone is killed in a road accident every two minutes?'
'I bet he gets awfully tired of it.'

'When I grow up I want to be a
ten-ton juggernaut.'
'Well I'm not going to stand in your way.'

A lorry carrying glue has overturned on the M6.
Police are warning motorists to stick to their
own lanes.

**Countless Cars Clog Carriageways,
Cause Chronic Coughs**

What car does Action Man drive?
A Toy-ota.

What car does an electrician drive?
A Voltswagen.

When is a car not a car?
When it turns into a garage.

What do you call a man under a car?
Jack.

What do you get if you cross a dog with
a four-wheel drive vehicle?
A Land Rover.

What goes 'crunk-crick'?
The seatbelt of a Japanese car.

What did the scoutmaster say when
his hooter was mended?
'Beep repaired.'

Why did the woman open the car door?
To let the clutch out.

How do we know there were cars
2000 years ago?
*Because Moses came over the
hill in Triumph.*

There was a sign outside a school:
DRIVERS TAKE CARE – DON'T KILL A
SCHOOLCHILD. Underneath someone had
added: WAIT FOR A TEACHER.

What part of a car causes the
most accidents?
The nut behind the wheel.

What car do big cats drive?
E-Type Jaguars.

What is a fjord?
A Norwegian motor car.

Where do Volkswagens go when they get
old and tattered?
The Old Volks home.

Why did the wally drive his car into
the lake?
He was trying to dip the headlights.

What has one horn and gives milk?
A milk lorry.

Did you hear about the wally who drove his car
over a cliff?
He wanted to test the air brakes.

'Are my car indicators working?'
'Yes, no, yes, no...'

A Martian spaceship landed in an empty petrol station and the leading Martian went straight up to the unleaded petrol pump and said, 'Take me to your leader'. There was no answer. 'Oi, mate', said the Martian, 'take your finger out of your ear when I'm talking to you.'

Why is a car out of petrol like dividing
20 by 7?
It won't go.

What car starts with T?
None – they all need petrol.

Fed Fearful Phosphates? Farmers Fault! (Gormless Gardeners Guilty? Greatly!)

What's the most popular gardening book?
Weeder's Digest.

What did the wally spy do when he found his
room was bugged?
He sprayed it with DDT.

What exams do farmers take?
Hay Levels.

Why was the farmer hopping mad?
Someone trod on his corn.

TEACHER: What are nitrates?
WALLY PUPIL: Er, the money you're paid for working late?

What is the difference between a market gardener and an actor?
One minds his peas, the other minds his cues.

Why did the farmer drive over his potato patch with a steam roller?
He wanted to grow mashed potatoes.

What do insects learn at school?
Mothematics.

What do you get if you cross a bug with
the Union Jack?
A patrio-tick.

What has tiny wings and is related to
the camel?
A hump-backed midge.

What makes the letter T so important to
a stick insect?
Without it, it would be a sick insect.

SID: Where do all the jungle bugs go
in winter?
JOE: Search me.
SID: No thanks, I just wanted to know.

What do you call an insect from
outer space?
Bug Rogers.

What did the earwig sing at the
football match?
'Earwigo, earwigo, earwigo...'

What can fly underwater?
A blue bottle in a submarine.

How do you keep flies out of the kitchen?
Put a bucket of manure in the bedroom.

Endangered Species

What's grey and wears a crown in the sea?
The Prince of Whales.

What do you get if you cross a whale with a nun?
Blubber and sister.

Where do you weigh a whale?
At a whale-weigh station.

MOTHER LION: What are you doing, son?
LION CUB: I'm chasing a poacher round
a tree.
MOTHER LION: How many times must
I tell you not to play with your food?

Did you hear about the lioness who got towed
away?
She parked on a yellow lion.

If a crocodile makes shoes, what does
a banana make.
Slippers!

Why is a camera like a crocodile?
Because they both snap.

What do you get if you cross a penguin with a
sheep?
A sheepskin dinner jacket.

What bird can write under water?
A ballpoint penguin.

What do you get if you cross an elephant with
the abominable snowman?
A jumbo yeti.

What transport do elephants use?
Ele-copters.

What's the fastest growing animal?
*The kangaroo – it grows in leaps
and bounds.*

What do you give a sick kangaroo?
A hoperation.

What do you get if you cross a bear with a
kangaroo?
A fur coat with large pockets.

What's the biggest species of mouse in
the world?
The hippopotamouse.

What's grey, heavy, and sends people
to sleep?
A hypnopotamus.

Why did the policeman cry?
Because he couldn't take his panda to bed with him.

What is black and white and has
eight wheels?
A panda on roller skates.

What do you call a reindeer with one eye?
No idea.

What do you call a reindeer that doesn't move,
and has one eye?
Still no idea.

What do you give a reindeer
with indigestion?
Elka-seltzer.

'Have you ever seen a man-eating tiger?'
'No, but I once saw a man eating chicken.'

How can you get a set of teeth put in
for free?
Smack a tiger.

What's white, furry, and smells
of peppermint?
A polo bear.

What do you call a polar bear in
ear-muffs?
Anything you like, it can't hear you.

Green and gone

What's green and sings?
Elvis Parsley.

What's green, wears a cloak and holds
up stagecoaches?
Dick Gherkin.

What's green, big and doesn't speak
all day?
The Incredible Sulk.

What's green and comes out of the ground
at 100 mph?
A Lettuce Elan.

What's green and hard?
A frog with a machine gun.

What's green, has two legs and a trunk?
A seasick holiday maker.

What goes green – amber – red?
A gooseberry in a temper.

What's green, yellow and red and
highly dangerous?
A two-ton parrot.

What's green and crisp and hard to
understand?
Lettuce think about it.

What's green, bent and indestructible?
The Six Million Dollar Cucumber.

What's green, has six legs, and would kill
you if it fell out of a tree?
A snooker table.